☛ W9-AZG-150

SILLY JOKES
COLORING BOOK

Edited by
Victoria Fremont

Illustrated by
Nina Barbaresi

DOVER PUBLICATIONS, INC.
New York

To Christopher and Jason

Copyright © 1991 by Dover Publications, Inc.
All rights reserved under Pan American and International Copyright Conventions.

Published in Canada by General Publishing Company, Ltd., 30 Lesmill Road, Don Mills, Toronto, Ontario.
Published in the United Kingdom by Constable and Company, Ltd., 3 The Lanchesters, 162–164 Fulham Palace Road, London W6 9ER.

Silly Jokes Coloring Book is a new work, first published by Dover Publications, Inc., in 1991.

International Standard Book Number: 0-486-26850-0

Manufactured in the United States of America
Dover Publications, Inc., 31 East 2nd Street, Mineola, N.Y. 11501

Note

If you and your friends love to tell jokes,
you know that sometimes the silliest jokes
are the most fun. There are 60 jokes in this
collection that are perfect for the silliest
moods. You and your friends can add to
the silliness and fun by coloring in all the
wacky illustrations any way you want
with pencils, pens, crayons or paints.

Did you hear about the teenage rooster?
He flew the coop.

ROBERT: I haven't slept in days.
JOHN: Why not?
ROBERT: Because I sleep at night.

Doctor, Doctor, I swallowed my kazoo!
Lucky you weren't playing your trumpet!

Doctor, Doctor, I need my head x-rayed!
Don't worry, they won't find anything.

Can I cook breakfast in my pajamas?
A frying pan is better.

Why does the moon go over the mountain?
It can't go under.

PEPPY: Coach, my doctor says I can't play ball.

COACH: Oh, he's seen you play, too.

MOTHER VAMPIRE: What's wrong?
BABY VAMPIRE: I just had a bitemare.

DAD: Hurry, I need to catch the train!
SON: Are you sure you're strong enough?

Will you always remember me?
Yes.
Let's play knock, knock. Knock, knock.
Who's there?
You didn't remember me!

EDDIE: I just got a toy boat for my brother.
RAY: Sounds like a good swap.

My friend has a thousand-pound gorilla.
Where does he sit?
Anywhere he wants.

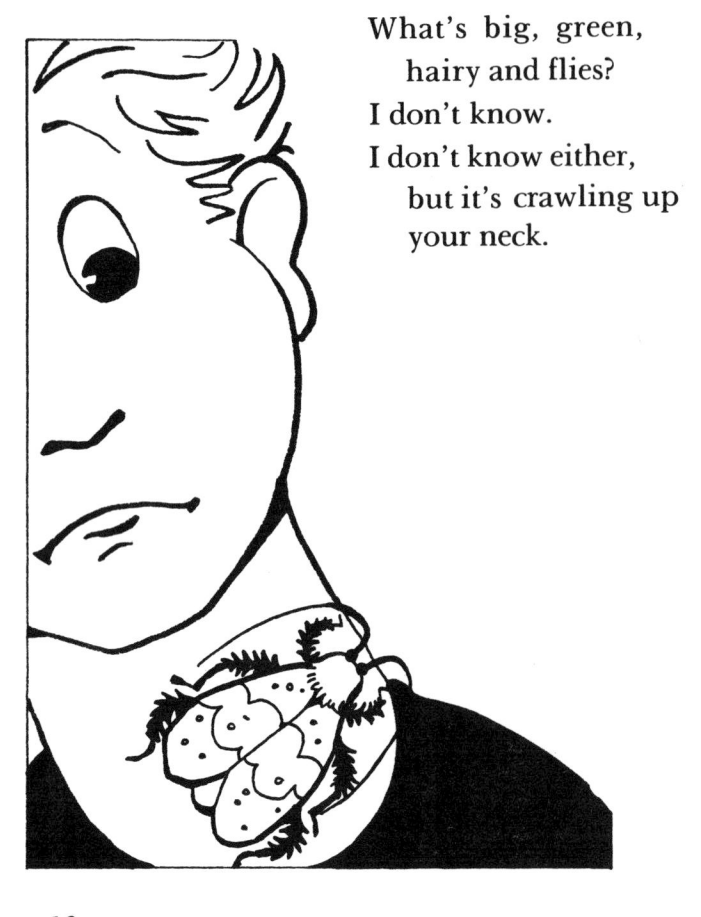

What's big, green,
    hairy and flies?
I don't know.
I don't know either,
    but it's crawling up
    your neck.

TEACHER: Chuck, what do
you think you'll be when
you grow up?
CHUCK: Very old.

What's white outside and furry inside?
A cat sandwich.

What should you do when a zebra turns blue?
Cheer him up.

Knock, knock.
Who's there?
Aich.
Aich who?
God bless you.

Did you hear the one about the ballplayer
  they put in jail?
He stole all the bases.

Did you hear the one about the tuna?
It's a fishy story.

Rachel reminds me of an egg.
Why's that?
She's always cracking up.

How does the ocean say hello to the beach?
It waves.

Did you hear the one about the airplane?
Never mind, it's over your head.

Knock, knock.
Who's there?
Little old lady.
Little old lady who?
I didn't know you could yodel!

RUFUS: I want a girlfriend who loves a good joke.

DAN: I can see why.

If ten cats were chasing one mouse, what time
would it be?
Ten after one.

Knock, knock.
Who's there?
Sal.
Sal who?
Sal long it's been good to know you.

Who did the frog call when he got a flat tire?
A toad truck.

TEACHER: What month has 28 days?
ALEX: They all do.

Did you hear about the two nuts that went
   out at night?
No, what happened?
One was a salted.

Knock, knock.
Who's there?
Police.
Police who?
Police let me in, I'm getting cold.

What did the monster say when he got a
　　stomachache?

"Must have been someone I ate."

Doctor, Doctor, I think I'm a bulldog!
How long have you thought that?
Ever since I was a puppy.

Doctor, Doctor, my husband thinks he's a
  cow!
Why didn't you tell me earlier?
We needed the milk.

Do you stir your tea with your right hand or
    your left hand?
Neither, I use a spoon.

Waiter, waiter, what's this fly doing in my
   soup?
Looks like the sidestroke, sir.

How do you make a chocolate shake?
Take it to a scary movie.

What did the mouse buy at the shoe store?
Squeakers.

How do you know carrots are good for your
 eyes?
Have you ever seen a rabbit with glasses?

Knock, knock.
Who's there?
Boo.
Boo who?
Why are you crying?

Waiter, is there spaghetti on the menu?
No, ma'am, I just wiped it off.

When is it time to go to the dentist?
Tooth-hurty.

What did the flea say when the puppy ran
away?
Doggone.

What do you get when you cross a skunk and
a baby?
A little stinker.

Did you hear the one about the baby?
It's a scream.

Did you hear the one about the rope?
Skip it.

What did one ghost say to the other?
Nice not to see you again.

What does Tarzan sing at
Christmas?
"Jungle Bells, Jungle Bells!"

A very fat man works
at the market.
Really? What does he weigh?
Fruits and vegetables.

How do you keep a rhinoceros from
   charging?
Take away its credit card.

What's a frog's favorite sport?
Croak-ay.

What did the wall say to the floor?
Meet me at the corner.

Doctor, Doctor, I ate a roll of film!
Relax, nothing bad will develop.

Why did Billy's father open a bakery?
He wanted to make some real dough.

CUSTOMER: I can't accept these pictures. My
  husband looks like an ape.
PHOTOGRAPHER: You picked him, I didn't.

TRAVELER: I'd like a room and a bath.

CLERK: I can give you a room, but you'll have to take your own bath.

Waiter, what's going on? There's an ant in
  my apple!
The worm's on vacation.

How did Rick beat his brother up?
Rick got up at six and his brother got up at
  seven.

TEACHER: Are you having a hard time with the questions?

SALLY: No, just the answers.

Did you hear about the fight in the bakery?
No.
Two rolls got fresh.

If I had ten oranges and I gave away three,
how many would I have left?
I don't know, in my class we use apples.